YOU CH

CAN YOU SURVIVE A

ZOMBIE APOCALYPSE?

An Interactive Doomsday Adventure

BY ANTHONY WACHOLTZ

ILLUSTRATED BY JAMES NATHAN

CAPSTONE PRESS
a capstone imprint

You Choose Books are published by Capstone Press,
1710 Roe Crest Drive, North Mankato, Minnesota 56003
www.capstonepub.com

Library of Congress Cataloging-in-Publication Data
Cataloging-in-publication information is on file with the Library of Congress.

ISBN 978-1-4914-5852-5 (library binding)
ISBN 978-1-4914-5925-6 (paperback)
ISBN 978-1-4914-5937-9 (eBook PDF)
ISBN 978-1-4914-7876-9 (reflowable Epub)

Editorial Credits
Mandy Robbins, editor; Bobbie Nuytten, designer; Jo Miller, media researcher;
Kathy McColley, production specialist; Nathan Gassman, creative director

Photo Credits
Dreamstime: Teh Soon Huat, 103, Shutterstock: Alex Malikov, 4, amgun,
(background, throughout), Esteban Die Ros, 109, greenga, 2-3, 4-5 (background),
photka, 106, rangizzz, 100

Printed and bound in the USA.
112016   010139R

TABLE of CONTENTS

ABOUT YOUR ADVENTURE

YOU are living a nightmare that has only been played out in scary stories and movies. The zombie apocalypse has become reality!

In this book you'll explore how the choices you make mean the difference between life and death. The events you'll experience haven't happened yet, but perhaps some day they will.

Chapter One sets the scene. Then you choose which path to read. Follow the directions at the bottom of each page. The choices you make will change your outcome. After you finish your path, go back and read the others for new perspectives and more adventures.

YOU CHOOSE THE PATH YOU TAKE THROUGH A ZOMBIE APOCALYPSE.

SURVIVING THE UNDEAD

"Daaaaad, don't sing along with the radio!"

Your dad agreed to drive you and two of your friends, Chloe and Logan, to the movie theater for an evening show. But you didn't know he would embarrass you this much.

"Since when are The Beatles not cool?" he asks with a smile.

You roll your eyes as your friends snicker from the backseat. You turn off the radio and are about to say something when a convoy of camouflaged army trucks speed by in the opposite direction.

You turn to look at your dad. "Did you see that?"

"It's probably just a training … "

Your dad stops mid-sentence and brings the car to a halt. He grips the steering wheel with both hands as his eyes go wide.

Turn the page.

You follow his gaze and see an elderly man attacking a young woman half a block down the street. The man thrashes at the woman with both hands and snaps his teeth. The terrified woman screams while trying to fend him off.

The two tumble to the ground as the woman fights to keep the man off her. Your dad opens the car door and turns to you. "Don't leave the car, no matter what happens," he says.

Before your dad can reach the struggle, the man sinks his teeth into the woman's upper arm. She lets out a blood-curdling wail as your dad kicks the man off of her. Before the man can get up, a group of people tackle him and pin him to the ground. The man gnashes his teeth together, grinding something in his mouth. You feel sick to your stomach when you realize it's the bite he took from the woman's arm.

"That's Mr. Miller! He owns the appliance store downtown," says Logan.

"He took a bite out of that woman!" cried Chloe.

Your dad runs back to the car and pops the trunk. He races around the car and grabs the first aid kit from the back. You stick your head out the window.

"Dad, what happened?" you ask.

"I … I don't know. Just stay in the car!"

He sprints back to the woman and starts to wrap her wound. As he secures the bandage, chaos breaks out in the crowd behind him. People start shoving each other and running in all directions. Your dad does his best to shield the injured woman.

"We have to go out there and help before the crowd stampedes them!" says Chloe.

"We should stay here," says Logan. "That's what your dad told us to do. Besides, we'll end up getting hurt ourselves."

To defend your dad on the street, turn to page 10.
To stay in the car, turn to page 43.

You don't care what your dad said. You look back at your friends. "Let's go," you say. "We have to at least try to help him."

Logan jumps out of the car and starts running down the street. You and Chloe are in close pursuit. But with the panicked crowd surging in the opposite direction, you can't see your dad anymore. A screaming man pushes Logan to the ground as he hurls by. You try to help Logan up but are knocked to the ground yourself. Chloe gets both of you back on your feet, and you push forward into the crowd.

"I can't find him!" you yell.

Logan grabs your arm and points to a small pool of blood on the street. "This is where they were!"

Your eyes linger on the blood for a moment before searching the crowd. There's no way you'll be able to find your dad in the chaos.

Turn the page.

"Don't you guys see what's happening?" says Logan. "Mr. Miller bit that woman. There's only one explanation for that."

Chloe rolls her eyes. "One person is bitten, and you're already talking about zombies? It's just one crazy person. We should report it to the police."

"No, no, no," says Logan. "If I'm right, going downtown is the last thing we want to do. We should get out of the city."

"Leave the city? Why would we do that?" you ask.

Logan looks you directly in the eyes. "If they are zombies, we'll want to go to a place that's not heavily populated. Zombies are drawn to people, to noise. We should head to the woods on the east side of town. It's only a couple miles away."

"Because of what you've seen in all those zombie movies?" Chloe asks, annoyed. "Even if you're right, the police station is the safest place for us now."

To get out of town, go to page 13.
To go to the police station, turn to page 66.

"If Logan's right, we should get away from large groups of people," you say. "The people here are getting crazier by the minute. Let's go back to my house. It's not far. Maybe Dad made it back there. Either way, we can grab some supplies at my house."

"Sounds good to me," Logan says. "But we should take the car. My mom is teaching me how to drive, and it's faster and safer than being on the street."

You head back to the car and jump in. Logan slowly turns the car around, avoiding the people in the street. You're facing the right direction, but you're not moving very fast.

"Uh, Logan? Any time now," you say.

"Your dad's a lot taller than me! Give me a second to move the seat up."

Chloe screams as a middle-aged man pounds frantically on the back driver's side door. A terrified young woman smacks the window on the other side of the car. Both are yelling, but you can't make out what they're saying. *Turn the page.*

13

"GO, GO, GO!" yells Chloe.

Logan slams his foot on the pedal, and the tires squeal as the car shoots forward. You swerve back and forth down the street before Logan regains control.

"People are crazy!" cries Chloe. "Maybe you were right, Logan. I'll bet the police station is a zoo right now."

You nod and point at the intersection ahead. "Turn right at the next stop sign."

"Yeah, I know how to get to your place. Let's go over what we're going to take with us now so we can get in and out."

"I'll grab the tent from my room," you say. "You guys pack some food and the gallon jug of water that's in the fridge. There's also a lighter in the kitchen drawer underneath the silverwa— "

Your words catch in your throat as Logan pulls up to your house. The front door is wide open.

Everyone is silent. You play out a dozen scenarios in your head on why your front door would be left open. None of them are good.

"We need to see if my mom is inside," you say.

The three of you get out of the car and cautiously walk into the house, stopping in the kitchen.

"Mom?" you say loudly, hoping for a response but not getting one.

"I'm sure she's okay," says Logan, unconvincingly, "but we should grab the supplies and head to the woods like we first planned."

"You're right," you say. "I'll grab the tent and leave her a note."

On the way to your room, you pass by the doorway to the basement. Muffled sounds rise up the stairs. It could be your mom, but the noises sound odd. You want to run downstairs to see, but maybe you should call out first.

To call out for your mom, turn to page 16.
To go downstairs, turn to page 20.

"Mom? Are you down there?"

There's no response, and the noise you heard before has stopped. You wonder if you should go downstairs, but you're glad you didn't. A face appears at the bottom of the stairs, but it's not your mom. It's a man with tattered clothes, scratches on his face, and blood smeared around his mouth.

The man lumbers up the stairs with an inhuman snarl. You slam the door, turn around, and slide to the floor with your back against the door. "Chloe! Logan!"

Your friends run out of the kitchen and give you a puzzled look. As the top of the basement door surges open, Logan rushes forward and pushes back.

"Chloe, grab the tent out of my room!" you yell. "It's under my bed!"

Chloe runs off without a word as you and Logan struggle to keep the basement door shut. You can hear the zombie on the other side—his growls are getting angrier by the second.

Turn the page.

Chloe reappears with the tent. "Let's push the couch in front of the door so we can make a run for it!"

Logan dashes to the couch and pulls while Chloe pushes. You feel the door open again, but you plant your feet and use your back to slam it shut. You wait a second before dodging out of the way as Chloe and Logan position the couch in front of the door.

"That's not going to hold long," you say. "Let's go."

Logan grabs a back pack he has stuffed with food as you hoist the tent under your arm. But before you take another step, four zombies stagger through the front door. You only have a moment to decide which way to run.

To run for the back door, go to page 19.
To run upstairs, turn to page 22.

You race out the back door and stop short. Your neighbors have stumbled out of their house. Drool oozes from their mouths as they stare at you hungrily. They stand between you and the car.

"We're going to have to walk," you mumble.

You make your way through streets swarming with panicked people. The crowd thins as you reach the woods. After an hour, you get to a clearing. Logan surveys the area and sets the tent down.

"Let's camp here. We can put sticks around the tent so we can hear if anything get close."

"Let's build a fire," says Chloe. "I'm cold."

"Chloe, if there are any zombies nearby, the light from the flames will draw them to us," says Logan. "Absolutely no fires."

Logan has a good point, but you are deep in the woods. You doubt anyone—or anything—from town would even see the flames.

To convince Logan to start a fire, turn to page 23.
To convince Chloe not to start a fire, turn to page 30.

You step lightly down the stairs and hear the noise again. You ease around the corner and see a man on his knees. He's hovering over a woman you've never seen before. From the sickening way the man rips at the flesh, you can tell he's a zombie. The woman must have run into the house seeking shelter and got trapped in the basement.

CRASH! A metallic clang echoes from above. One of your friends dropped something in the kitchen! The zombie jerks its head upward toward the ceiling. You freeze in place and hold your breath, but the zombie's eyes dart in your direction. You turn to run, but a bony hand grabs your leg. You squirm and kick, but its fingers dig in like talons. You cry out in pain as the zombie bites down on your bare ankle. You lose the strength to pull away with each bite. It's only a matter of time before you turn into one of the undead.

THE END

To follow another path, turn to page 9.
To read the conclusion, turn to page 101.

You drop the tent and run to the stairs, climbing them three at a time with Chloe and Logan right behind you. You reach the hallway at the top and dash to your bedroom. Once all three of you are inside, you slam the door shut. Chloe and Logan move your dresser in front of the door seconds before fists pound on the other side.

Through your window, you see dozens of zombies stumbling through your lawn. "I think we're going to be here awhile," you say.

The food Chloe and Logan packed for the woods only lasts a couple days. After a week, your stomach rumbles nonstop, but the moans from the hallway keep you from venturing out to find food. The water runs out a few days later. You know you and your friends can only survive a couple more days, and you are losing hope that someone will come to your rescue.

THE END

To follow another path, turn to page 9.
To learn more about zombies, turn to page 101.

"We're going to freeze out here without a fire, Logan," you say. "We'll just make sure to keep it small."

Logan looks at the ground and shakes his head. "Do what you want, but don't blame me when zombies come barreling in like moths."

"How do you know so much about zombies?" you ask.

"Books, movies, documentaries. It fascinates me. I just never thought I would have to use the information."

You stack some wood into a pile as Logan continues. "Zombies only want one thing—to feed. They move slower than we do, but speed doesn't matter if you're facing a whole pack of zombies."

You start the kindling ablaze, and soon you have a toasty little fire going. The three of you stand around the flames as the sun dips completely out of view. The heat from the fire feels good, but now you have to put the tent together in the dark.

Turn the page.

"The fire's already going out," says Chloe. "I'm going to add a couple logs before we start on the tent."

You've put the tent together several times, but trying to explain the directions in the dark is difficult. Your frustration builds after making little progress in half an hour.

Bright light catches the corner of your eye. The bonfire! With everyone focusing on the tent, no one was watching the fire. The flames spew upward, at least 5 feet high. The fire lights up the faces of a zombie horde stumbling through the trees toward you.

"Let's make a run for it!" whispers Chloe.

"We'll never get past them all," you reply. "We could climb a tree and wait it out. Zombies can't climb trees, so maybe they'll lose interest and wander off."

"But if they don't," says Logan, "we'll be stuck up there."

To climb a tree, turn to page 26.
To make a run for it, turn to page 27.

You'd rather take your chances in a tree than dodge the outstretched hands of a dozen zombies. You take a few steps and leap for the nearest branch. Within seconds, you've scrambled to a safe height.

That's when you notice Logan and Chloe didn't follow you. They've rushed through a small gap in the zombies. One of them grabs the hood of Chloe's sweatshirt. She squirms out of it, and both she and Logan run out of sight with several zombies in pursuit.

However, most of the zombies have followed you to the tree. They swarm the trunk with arms stretched high, scraping at the bark and moaning hungrily. You hug the trunk for balance as hours slip by. Night turns to day, and day turns to night, but Chloe and Logan haven't returned. Your arms grow tired from clutching the trunk. Sadly, the zombies never seem to tire. You wonder if help will ever come.

THE END

To follow another path, turn to page 9.
To learn more about zombies, turn to page 101.

"Let's go for it," you say. "There's a small gap in the zombies behind us."

You turn and dash between two zombies behind you. Both of them reach for you, but you avoid their grasp. Logan starts to follow you, but the zombies have already closed the gap. He cuts to the right and around one of the zombies, narrowly missing the decaying, outstretched arm of a third zombie.

Chloe tries to follow Logan, but the third zombie snares the hood of her sweatshirt. She starts to wrestle out of it, but her head gets stuck as she struggles to get her arms out. A muffled scream flows through the sweatshirt as another zombie grabs an empty sleeve.

Chloe pulls away but stumbles, swinging around the two zombies and losing her balance. As she crashes to the ground, her head and arms fall free from the sweatshirt. She jumps to her feet, and the three of you sprint through the trees.

Turn the page.

The moon gives just enough light for you to dodge hanging branches. After half an hour, you hear moving water. You stop in front of a narrow river.

"UHRRR!"

You jump back, startled. A zombie writhes on the ground not more than 15 feet in front of you. Its right foot is snagged in the forked base of a tree. Its mouth gapes open and snaps shut over and over as it tries unsuccessfully to crawl toward you.

"We should take it out," says Logan as he hands you a heavy branch. "We don't want it following us. Aim for the head."

You look at him with an odd expression. "What?" he asks. "Haven't you ever seen a zombie movie? If you shoot a zombie in the chest or hack off a limb, it still comes at you. Remove the head, kill the zombie."

You know the creature isn't human, but you still feel nauseous at the thought of taking a swing at it.

To swing the branch at the zombie, turn to page 39.
To leave the zombie and continue on, turn to page 40.

"Chloe, if Logan's right, we should do whatever we can to not attract attention."

Chloe hangs her head but nods in agreement. The two of you start putting the tent together as Logan gathers sticks. Before long, you're pounding the last stake into the ground, and Logan is dropping sticks around the entrance to the tent. The sun is nearing the horizon. You head into the tent, and Logan breaks out the food from the backpack.

"I still don't think we're dealing with zombies," says Chloe. "But if there are zombies out there, we'll need to take turns on watch. I'm exhausted, so I would rather not take the first watch."

Logan turns to you and shrugs. "It's up to you."

To take the first watch, go to page 31.
To let Logan have the first watch, turn to page 35.

Chloe and Logan settle into their sleeping bags. You and Logan take turns guessing what caused the zombie outbreak. Before long, you're the only one awake.

If you're going to keep watch, you'd rather do it outside the tent so you can see what's coming. You quietly step over Logan, unzip the tent, and sneak out. You arch your back and stretch, looking up at the stars poking through the trees. A pale glow from the moon peeks through the branches. Carefully stepping over Logan's ring of twigs, you start to walk toward town while making sure you can still see the tent.

On a normal night, the only sound would be wind rustling through the leaves. But just faintly you can hear sounds that send chills down your spine. Honking horns. Occasional gunfire. Bloodcurdling screams. Maybe Logan was right—you're better off away from the city.

Turn the page.

You turn around, but the tent is nowhere in sight. You must have walked farther than you thought. You make your way back to the tent, keeping your eyes focused on the ground to avoid stepping on anything that would make noise. As you get close to the tent, you hear twigs snapping. Your eyes catch something moving 15 feet in front of the tent. A zombie!

You freeze mid-step. The zombie hasn't seen you or the tent, but you start to panic when you realize you left the tent flap wide open. If Chloe or Logan make the slightest sound, the zombie will be on top of them in seconds.

There's no way to warn them now. You could stay still and hope the zombie passes. The only other option is to try to lead the zombie away from the tent.

To stay still, go to page 33.
To draw the zombie's attention, turn to page 36.

You decide to stay quiet and wait it out. Hopefully the zombie will move away from the tent so you can warn your friends. Each minute seems like an hour as you watch the zombie stare into the darkness, lumber a few steps, and stare again.

Finally the zombie starts to lurch away from the camp. You let out a tiny sigh of relief. You can't wait to tell your friends about the close encounter.

"Hey! Are you out here?"

Your heart sinks as Logan steps out of the tent. The zombie stops dead in its tracks. You're about to yell out to warn him when a searing pain rips through your neck. You were so focused on the zombie near the tent that you didn't notice the one coming up behind you. Your fate is sealed, but you hope your friends will make it out of the woods alive.

THE END

To follow another path, turn to page 9.
To learn more about zombies, turn to page 101.

You're exhausted, so you let Logan take the first watch and fall into a fitful sleep. Suddenly gnarled hands grasp at you from all directions. Gaping mouths pour out putrid breath into your face. Teeth clash together in a repeating, frenzied motion.

You sit up with a start as a scream escapes your lips. You're in a cold sweat, and your heart is racing. You heave a sigh of relief when you realize it was just a nightmare!

Your relief quickly fades when you see the look of horror on Logan's face. The silence breaks as sticks crackle and snap around your tent. Urgent, ghastly moans fill the air as Logan tries to quietly wake Chloe. As the zombies claw at the tent, you realize you have doomed yourself and your friends.

THE END

To follow another path, turn to page 9.
To learn more about zombies, turn to page 101.

You pick up a large stick and walk toward the zombie. When you're 15 feet away, you smack the branch against a nearby tree. The zombie's head spins, and in an awkward pivot, it turns and staggers toward you in a single motion. You step backward slowly and hit another tree with the stick, making sure the zombie stays focused on you. You lead the zombie over a hill so that the tent is out of sight.

Hollow moans sprout up behind you. Six more zombies are feasting on a deer, but their eyes grow wide with fresh prey in sight.

Before you can run, the zombie you led from the camp falls over in front of you. Bewildered, you spin around and watch as the other zombies topple over, one by one.

Turn the page.

With a slight rustle, four soldiers emerge out of the brush. Each is wearing night-vision goggles and carrying a silenced pistol.

"Are you hurt?" one of them asks you. "Did they touch you?"

"No," you say. "Thanks for saving me!"

"Are you alone out here?" he asks.

"No. My two friends are back at the tent," you reply.

You lead the soldiers over the hill to the tent. You wake up Chloe and Logan, who are groggy at first but are jolted awake at the sight of the soldiers. The soldiers lead you to an evacuation site with helicopters and many heavily armed soldiers. As you pass over the city, you see crowds of people rushing through the streets, cars piled up in accidents, and fires stretching across entire blocks. You're just glad you made it out alive.

THE END

To follow another path, turn to page 9.
To learn more about zombies, turn to page 101.

You step toward the zombie and swing the large branch up over your head. The momentum makes you lose your balance, and you crash to the ground.

Logan and Chloe grab your wrists, but the zombie has your calf. Its leg is still wedged in the tree, and neither of you are budging.

The noise has attracted more zombies. You look up at Chloe and Logan. "Run!" you yell. "Leave me!"

Logan shakes his head furiously, but you twist your arms free of their grasp. "Go! NOW!" Finally Chloe grabs Logan's hand and pulls him away from you.

Your attention goes back to the zombie clawing at your pants. You kick at the zombie with your free leg, struggling to break from its grasp. But you know that even if you do, you won't be able to escape the oncoming zombies.

THE END
To follow another path, turn to page 9.
To learn more about zombies, turn to page 101.

"Let's just leave him there," you say. "He's not going anywhere."

Less than 50 yards down the river, a fallen tree stretches from one bank to the other. "Let's cross there," says Logan. "Then we can follow the river north until we reach a highway."

Logan and Chloe hoist themselves up on the tree. You wait until Chloe crawls a few feet before you climb up. You wrap your legs around the tree as much as you can and use your arms to scoot forward. You're not moving very quickly, but you're confident you won't end up in the river.

"Uh-oh … "

You look up at Logan and follow his gaze. A zombie sitting at the base of a tree across the river has just seen you. It moans, struggling to get to its feet. At the same time, you hear a cry come from behind you. The zombie that was stuck has climbed on to the fallen tree.

Turn the page.

"Keep going," you say. "We have a better shot on the other side of the river."

By the time Logan nears the end of the tree, the zombie is waiting for him. The zombie stretches its arms toward Logan's foot. Logan thrashes and kicks at the zombie, but that only seems to anger it.

Just as the zombies' fingers curl around Logan's shoe, its eyes go wide and its body falls to the ground. A camouflaged soldier stares at the unmoving zombie a moment before wiping his knife on the grass and putting it back in its sheath. "You kids OK?" he asks.

You're speechless. Chloe's mouth gapes open in shock. "T-t-thanks," stammers Logan.

The soldier explains that he was separated from his group but knows where the evacuation site is. He leads you through the woods to a clearing and helps you into a helicopter. You can only hope you're headed somewhere safe and free of the undead.

THE END

To follow another path, turn to page 9.
To learn more about zombies, turn to page 101.

Your dad's hands are full trying to help the woman, and you don't want to add to his problems.

"Let's stay here," you say. "My dad knows what he's doing."

You lock the doors and turn the radio back on in case there are any reports about what's happening. You flip from station to station as you keep an uneasy eye on the growing crowd outside the car. You stop when you hear an authoritative voice come on the radio.

" ... are unsure of what caused the situation. We do know the southeast part of the city has seen multiple outbreaks. We urge citizens to stay in their houses and lock their doors."

You look back at your friends. "He said 'outbreak.' Does that mean there's a serious virus spreading around or what?"

Logan shrugs. "Who knows? Let's keep listening."

Turn the page.

BAM! BAM! BAM!

You jump as a frantic man bangs on one of the car windows. He grasps the door handle with both hands and pulls in a heaving motion. Chloe lets out a scream as a woman appears in another side window. You can't make out her shouts, but you know that both people want to get inside the car.

"Should we let them in?" asks Chloe.

"No!" yells Logan. "If there is a virus outbreak, they might be infected."

You look out the windshield, but the crowd has grown so thick you can no longer see your dad. You know you missed your opportunity to help him, and now you're worried about your own safety too.

To let the people inside the car, turn to page 46.
To drive away, turn to page 54.

Before Logan can object, you unlock the doors and wave the people inside. The man climbs into the driver's seat, and the woman slides in next to Chloe in the back.

"Thanks!" says the woman. "It's not safe out there."

"We can go wherever you want," says the man. "We just needed to get away from the crowd."

You turn to Chloe and Logan. "I'd like to go to my house. My mom might be there, and I'm hoping my dad finds his way there."

They both nod, so you turn to face the man. "We can drop you off at the library. It's not far from my house."

"Sure thing," he replies. He turns the car around, moving slowly to avoid hitting the crowd.

After a few blocks, the woman asks, "Have any of you heard what's happening?"

"No, we were just heading to a movie," says Chloe. "Then this crazy guy attacked and bit someone on the street."

"Are you kidding?" says the man. "I was bit on the hand by someone as I walked to work this morning. I called the police, but the line was busy for more than an hour. I walked over there on my lunch break, but they've got a barricade blocking all entrances to the building. I've never seen anything like it." The man shakes his bandaged hand. "Geez ... my hand still really hurts."

You turn around in your seat. Chloe, Logan, and the woman look at you with wide eyes.

To ask the man to stop the car, turn to page 48.
To continue on to the library, turn to page 49.

"Can you stop here?" you ask the man. "We should … ask around about what caused the panic."

The man looks at his hand, then at you. "What are you talking about?"

Before you can assure the man, Logan chimes in from the back seat. "I am NOT staying in a car with a future zombie."

The man slams on the brakes and turns to Logan. "It's just a bite! Zombies aren't real! You don't know what you're talking about!"

You look back at Chloe, who gives you a frightened and uncertain look. Through a flurry of hand signals, you explain to Chloe and the woman to open the doors and get out. You pull the handle and push your shoulder into the door. As it swings open, two zombies rush toward you, blocking your escape. Screams fill the car as the zombies pile on top of you.

THE END

To follow another path, turn to page 9.
To learn more about zombies, turn to page 101.

Unsure what to say back to the man, you face forward and remain quiet. The car becomes silent except the repeating radio announcement. The man flexes his hand a few more times, and you do your best not to stare.

Logan pulls at your sleeve between the car door and your seat. You turn your head slightly as he leans in. "Another bite? We're definitely dealing with zombies. There's no telling how long it will be before he turns. It all depends on how long ago he was bitten and how deep the bite went."

You look at him through the side rear view mirror and raise your eyebrows, as if to say, "What can we do?"

Turn the page.

A couple minutes later, the car starts to drift. The man jerks the steering wheel and gets the car in the lane again. He shakes his head from side to side and grips the steering wheel tightly. After a few more blocks, the car swerves again, but this time you stray further into the other lane. By this time, the man has one eye closed, and the other flutters open as he twitches.

"Sir?" you ask shakily.

He slowly turns his head to you, drool spilling out of his mouth. He gags, and his hands fall off the steering wheel. The car fills with screams as you veer off the road. You jump the curb and smash into a car parked in a driveway. The force throws your head and arms forward, but your seat belt holds you in place.

Turn the page.

"Is everyone OK?" you ask. You try to turn in your seat, but you're sore from the crash.

"Yeah, we're OK," replies Chloe. Your two friends and the woman crawl out of the back seat, but the man lies motionless behind the wheel.

"Sir? Are you okay?" you ask, gently shaking the man's shoulder. He doesn't move.

You push the car door open and put your left hand on the seat to help propel you out.

"OWWW!" The man has clamped his teeth down on your wrist. You jerk backward, ripping your hand from his teeth and falling out of the car in the process. You stand up, touching your wrist gently. He broke the skin in several places.

The man snarls at you from the car, but the seat belt is keeping him from coming at you.

Chloe rushes over. "Your hand!"

Logan keeps his distance, looking at you hesitantly. "You've been bitten," he says solemnly. The woman takes one look at you before she turns and runs off.

"We need to get you to a hospital!" urges Chloe.

"No!" shouts Logan. "The hospital will be filled with other people who have been bitten, and some of them have probably already turned."

"Turned? What do you mean turned?" asks Chloe.

"Become zombies," he replies. "One bite, one scratch from a zombie … that's all it takes to become one."

"I don't care," she says. "He needs help. The hospital is only a few blocks away."

"We're close to my house too," you say. "I'll bet my mom will know what to do."

To go to your house, turn to page 56.
To go to the hospital, turn to page 58.

You climb into the driver's seat and shift the car into gear. You slowly roll forward, but the man punches and cracks your window. You panic, slamming your foot down on the gas pedal. You speed up, but after a couple blocks, you jerk the wheel to avoid the crowd. You crash into a tree, and the airbag slams you back into your seat.

You're pinned in place, but you manage to open the driver's door. Most of the crowd is running away from you, but several people are stumbling toward your open car door. Their sickly gray skin is torn and scratched. Wailing moans drift out of their gaping mouths.

"Zombies!" Logan yells from the back seat. You watch helplessly as a zombie bites deep into your forearm. A second zombie bites your neck. The pain is more than you can take, and you black out. When you come to, you'll be roaming the streets as a zombie.

THE END

To follow another path, turn to page 9.
To learn more about zombies, turn to page 101.

You run to your house. When you get there, the front door is open. You run inside and search for your parents. As you reach the basement stairs, a disgusting smell wafts up from below.

You creep downstairs and find two bodies on the floor. Your dad stands over them holding a bat. When he sees you, he rushes over and embraces you tightly.

"I'm so glad you made it home!" he cries. "I tried to get back to the car, but I got stuck in the crowd. I came back here, hoping to find you and your mom." He gestures toward the men on the floor. "I wasn't able to save him … the zombie got to him first." Suddenly his eyes drop to your hand. "No … "

Logan and Chloe rush downstairs. They stop short when they see your dad's expression.

"C'mon," says your dad as he grabs your other hand. "Some people were talking about a military medical base on the edge of town. Maybe they can do something for you. Mom's car is in the garage."

After hours of traffic, you pull up to the base, and a soldier flags you down. "Has anyone in here been bitten or scratched?" he barks.

"Yes, my child has been bitten," your dad responds, gesturing to you. Immediately, your door opens and two soldiers drag you out.

"Hey! Stop!" yells your dad. A man in a lab coat walks over to you and hands you a bottle of water. "Sorry for the rough welcome," he says. "But we're in a bit of a time crunch. I'm Dr. Bachmann."

"What do you want with me?" you stammer.

"You've been bitten," the man replies. "But we've been working on an antidote to the—virus, let's say—that is passed on through blood contact with a zombie. We need to test it to know if it works."

"You want me to be a guinea pig …"

"Yes. If the antidote works, no one else would become a zombie."

To refuse the antidote, turn to page 61.
To let him to test the antidote on you, turn to page 63.

"I need to get my hand checked out, Logan," you say, holding it out to him. "It looks bad, doesn't it?"

He stares at your hand a moment and nods. "All right, let's go."

You arrive at the hospital to find a scene of complete pandemonium. People are lined up outside the doors, wailing to be let in. Abandoned cars block the emergency room entrance. An ambulance with its sirens blaring tries to get into the parking lot but smashes into a light post.

A nurse walks along the line of people, trying to maintain order. You rush up to her as she addresses a woman with a bandaged head.

Turn the page.

"Excuse me," says Chloe. "Can you please have someone look at his bite?"

As soon as Chloe says "bite," the nurse whirls around. Her eyes fall to your hand, then your face. She looks at you with tired, swollen eyes. Her lips are pressed tightly together. "I'm sorry—there's nothing I can do."

You're about to ask what she means when a teenager in line screams. The person next to her has ripped out a piece of her forearm with his teeth. He bites down again, this time clamping onto her wrist. The nurse runs to the girl and pulls her free. At the same moment, another person bites down on the nurse's leg. You're about to run when several hands pull you to the ground. Your last thoughts are of your mom and dad—you hope they survive the zombie apocalypse.

THE END

To follow another path, turn to page 9.
To learn more about zombies, turn to page 101.

"An experimental antidote?" you ask. "I don't know if that's a good idea. Does it matter that I was bitten almost five hours ago?"

"Five hours? Well, we've only tested recently affected people so far. Within the first hour or two."

It sounds awfully risky. You turn down the offer. Dr. Bachmann looks disappointed and angry, but he respects your decision. "Then we need to do what we can to slow down the zombification process."

Two soldiers wheel a gurney and medical equipment through the tent flaps. You switch into a hospital gown and lie down. A woman in a lab coat puts an IV in your arm.

"We're going to sedate you," she explains. "Your body will slow down and buy us some time."

Before long, your eyes grow heavy, and you fall asleep.

Your parents are the first thing you see when you open your eyes. Tears flow down their faces.

Turn the page.

"How do you feel?" your mom asks.

You smack your lips. Your mouth is incredibly dry. "My hand hurts, but I feel OK. How long have I been out?"

Dr. Bachmann appears on the other side of the gurney. "Three days," he says. "I'm glad to hear you're doing well. The soreness in your hand will last a few days, but you're extremely lucky. We tested the original antidote on another bite victim with a similar infection timeline. He experienced some rather disturbing side effects. Our scientists tweaked the antidote, and your parents agreed to test it on you."

"And it worked," finished your dad, a huge smile on his face. "They've set up a place for us to stay while they monitor you."

You can't believe you were bitten by a zombie and survived. You hope they can distribute the antidote fast enough to stop the zombie outbreak.

THE END

To follow another path, turn to page 9.
To learn more about zombies, turn to page 101.

"Let's go for it," you say.

Dr. Bachmann smiles. "Great," he says, holding up a syringe. "You'll feel a sting, not unlike a flu shot."

You lay down on a gurney, and Dr. Bachmann inserts the needle into your arm. You watch the light blue fluid drain out of the syringe as he pushes the plunger down. A cool sensation rushes through your arm and throughout the rest of your body.

Dr. Bachmann removes the needle and sets it on a table. "Now we wait," he says. "We should see results in 24 hours or less."

Two soldiers step from the corner of the tent and tether your arms and legs to the table. Dr. Bachmann sees your concerned face. "Sorry—it's just a precaution."

You don't know if it's antidote or plain exhaustion, but you're soon fast asleep. When you wake up, your head is pounding, and your entire body aches.

Turn the page.

"Doctor …"

Dr. Bachmann rushes to the table as you turn your head and vomit. Your stomach cramps again, and you pull against your restraints.

"Johnson! Meyers! Get over here now!"

Two soldiers rush forward to pin your arms down, but you surge forward, breaking free of the tethers around your wrists. You grab one of the soldiers as he approaches and sink your teeth into his neck. Dr. Bachmann and the other soldier run from the room.

The antidote was a failure, but there's only thing on your mind now—human flesh.

THE END
To follow another path, turn to page 9.
To learn more about zombies, turn to page 101.

"Chloe's right," you say. "And even if they are zombies, the police station would be the safest place in town. I just hope we find my dad on the way."

"Fine. But we should take the car," says Logan. "I can drive. Well, I've been practicing with my mom. It's only a few blocks, but I'd rather not walk there."

You agree—people are becoming more and more frantic. You get back to the car, and Logan reaches for the driver's door. Suddenly, a middle-aged woman grabs him by the shoulder and tosses him to the ground.

"Hey!" yells Logan, as the woman climbs into the car and peels out in reverse. People from the crowd dive out of the way as she turns the wheel too hard and smashes into a parked car. Angry people from the crowd run to the car and start pounding on the windshield. You've seen enough—it's time to go.

The police station is only six blocks away, but the progress is slow. Traffic has come to a halt. People have flooded the streets in an attempt to flee the city. Shouting fills the air, mixed with an occasional shriek or revving engine. You and your friends stick to the sidewalk, staying as close to the buildings as possible.

After a few blocks, the chaos on the streets is incredibly worse. Nonstop screaming drowns out most of the other noise. Attacks similar to the one you witnessed with Mr. Miller are happening all over. The look in the eyes of the people doing the biting chills you to your core. There's no doubt in your mind now—those people are zombies.

You finally reach the police station, but you run into a barricade of cruisers and a chain-link metal fence. People desperately cling to the fence, begging to be let in even though no one is on the other side.

Turn the page.

You overhear a man talking to a small group of people near the fence. "There's a safe zone on the northwest side of the city," he says. "They have armed military personnel guarding a base filled with food, water, and everything else you'd need."

Logan grabs your shoulder and pulls you and Chloe away from the crowd. "We'll never make it in a crowd," he says. "Look—Chloe found a small gap in the fence. We're going to crawl through and go down the alley. There might be a way into the police station back there."

*To follow the small group to the safe zone,
go to page 69.*
*To go through the fence with Logan and Chloe,
turn to page 72.*

"We should stick with the crowd," you say. "There's safety in numbers."

Logan gives you a frustrated look, but Chloe tugs his arm and says, "C'mon. We're not splitting up."

You go back to the group, which has nearly tripled in size. "All right, let's go!" someone shouts, and the group breaks away from the fence and toward the northwest side of town. After only two blocks, the group has become a crowd, with more and more people joining in as you go.

However, the size of the group has attracted several zombies. As people on the edges of the crowd are bit, a shrill cry rings out in the street. The crowd turns into a raging mob, and the people are now stampeding away from the zombies.

Turn the page.

In the panic, a man runs into you, and your legs become tangled with his. You both sprawl out on the street, but the crowd pays no notice. You curl into a ball and cover your head with your arms as the pounding steps of the mob rush over you. You hear a sickening crack as someone steps on your leg.

The mob finally passes over you. Chloe and Logan are nowhere in sight. You try to move, but immense pain shoots up your leg, which is probably broken. The man who ran into you is gasping for air and clutching his side. He probably has several broken ribs, but he still lets out a scream as a zombie falls on top of him and bites his arm.

You look up and see several more zombies lurching toward you. Unable to move, you'll meet the same fate as the man next to you.

THE END
To follow another path, turn to page 9.
To learn more about zombies, turn to page 101.

You follow Logan and Chloe through the gap in the fence and head down the alley. Three zombies are on their knees at the far end of the alley, but they don't notice you. You don't want to know what they are feasting on.

You reach the back door to the police station, but another chain-link fence blocks your way. A padlock secures it in place.

"Now what do we do?" whispers Chloe.

You turn back, but two zombies have found the gap in the fence. Another round of screams echoes down the alley, which causes the other zombies to look in your direction. The closest one stumbles forward, blood dripping from its mouth.

"There's no point in being quiet anymore," says Logan. He turns and grips the fence, shaking it violently. "Help! Help us!"

Logan's yells only seem to excite the zombies, who are staggering toward you at a quicker pace. But someone else has heard Logan.

A man in a police uniform steps up to the gate. "Have any of you been bitten?"

"No!" cries Chloe. "Please let us in!"

The police officer stares at you for a moment, then begins fumbling with the padlock. The zombies are closing in as you hear the padlock pop. The officer pulls the fence back and points toward the open back door of the police station. "Go! Now!"

Logan runs through first, but you and Chloe are close behind. As you run past, the officer starts to drag the fence back in place. But the zombies have already reached the fence.

"AAAAHHHH!"

The officer screams as one zombie bites him on his right hand. A second zombie has fallen to its knees and clamps its teeth around the officer's leg. Two more zombies push past the officer and come straight at you.

Turn the page.

"Shut the door!" screams Chloe.

You slam the door shut and lock it. A booming voice behind you makes you jump.

"What are you kids doing?" bellows a broad-shouldered man with a thick beard.

"Trying to survive!" Logan angrily responds.

"You just got Jake killed," says the man. "And with the fence unlocked, the only thing keeping the zombies out is that door."

"Maybe if you would have gone out there to help him, he would be standing here with us right now," challenges Logan.

Tempers are flaring, and you know you should speak up. But who do you side with? You want to stick up for your friend, but the man has a valid point.

To defend Logan, turn to page 76.
To side with the man, turn to page 78.

"What were we supposed to do?" you ask the man angrily. "What would you have done in our position? The exact same thing!"

The man glares at you for a moment before storming off. A woman approaches you.

"Don't mind him," she says. "Jake was a friend of his. But what other choice did you have?"

"I'm glad you understand," you say. You scan the room, noticing wooden boards across the windows and furniture in front of the doors. A filing cabinet was moved away from the back door from when the police officer came to your rescue.

"You guys are prepared," says Chloe.

"I guess you could say that," says the woman. "I only live a block away, so when I saw the chaos in the street, the police station seemed like a natural choice. That was before things really got out of hand. C'mon, let me introduce you to the others."

You walk through a hallway to the main room of the station. Desks are pressed up against the doors in this room too. The bearded man is talking excitedly to the other people.

"This is our chance!" you overhear him say. "If we push those kids out the front door, the zombies will go after them. Then we can get out of here and head to the evacuation zone on the northwest side of town."

"You will do no such thing!" yells the woman as she puts her arm around you. "You're not going to sacrifice these kids just to save yourself."

"It's not up to you!" he sneers. "These people want to get to safety as much as I do."

Looking at the faces of the other people, you're not convinced they would stand up to the man. At best, they seem unsure of what to do with you. If you're going to plead your case, you better speak up now.

To try to reason with the man, turn to page 82.
To sneak away with your friends, turn to page 83.

"Logan, this man wouldn't have been able to do anything to help the police officer." You turn to the man. "The police officer saved our lives. We are grateful for that."

The man seems satisfied with your appreciation. But Logan is fuming. "Are you kidding me? This guy yells at us and you're siding with him?" Before you can respond, Logan storms off into the police station.

The man guides you down a hallway and into the main room of the station. He introduces you to the other five people and gives you water and a couple of granola bars.

"Feel free to look around, but don't go too far," he says. "We overheard a message on the police scanner about reaching an evacuation zone in the north part of town. As soon as we come up with a plan, we're outta here."

You and Chloe wander through a cluttered office, past a couple of bathrooms, and around the evidence locker. The next room, which has oversized lockers lining the walls, hooks up with the hallway near the back door. The gun lockers have already been cleared out. There's no sign of Logan.

You walk over to the TV on the wall. The president is giving an emergency State of the Union address. There is no podium or usual backdrop. The speech is happening aboard Air Force One. The president says that there is a pandemic that has swept the nation. He urges people to stay indoors and advises against going to the hospital. The address does little to calm your nerves.

"Let's head back to the main room," you say. "Hopefully Logan ended up there."

You walk into the hallway and hear the zombies pounding on the back door. Suddenly, the door flies open, and zombies fall over each other as they stumble through the door.

Turn the page.

Chloe starts to scream, but an arm reaches around her head and covers her mouth. You're pulled back into the locker room by Logan.

"Quick, hide in a locker," he whispers. "They can smell us, but they'll be more attracted to the noise in the main room."

You jump into the nearest locker and shut the door. Chloe and Logan do the same. Within seconds, zombies stumble into the locker room. You try to steady your fast-paced breathing, which isn't easy. You can see some filter down the hallway while the rest pass through the locker room. In less than a minute, you can hear screams from the main room.

Logan slowly comes out of his locker first, and you and Chloe follow suit. "We should try to help them," you say.

"We can't help them anymore," he says. "We have to leave the station now."

To follow Logan out the back door, turn to page 88.
To go to the main room of the station, turn to page 90.

"Look, we don't want any trouble," you say to the man. "If we're not welcome, we'll leave first chance we get."

"No!" shouts the man. "You three are our ticket out of here before the zombies swarm this place. You are going out the front door, and the rest of us are going to escape! That's what's going to happen!"

Everyone goes quiet at the sound of wood splintering. The man's shouts have attracted zombies on the side of the station. Two boards snap and break, revealing zombie heads leering through the windows. After a few hits, the first window shatters.

Glass flies as two windows on the other side of the room break. Zombies start climbing in through the windows. You run to the hallway, but zombies have already burst through the back door. There's nowhere to run now.

THE END

To follow another path, turn to page 9.
To learn more about zombies, turn to page 101.

The woman walks up to the man and talks with him angrily. While the man is distracted by the woman, you and your friends sneak back to the hallway.

"I'm not going to stick around and wait for their decision," says Chloe.

"If the zombies out back are still—focused—on the officer, maybe we can sneak around them," you say.

You put your ear to the back door, but you can't hear anything. You open the door slightly and see the police officer on the ground with seven zombies around him. You motion for Chloe and Logan to follow you.

The three of you pass the zombies. You're about to leave when you notice Logan left the back door open. When the zombies are finished with the officer, they'll wander right into the station.

You should go back and shut the door, but Chloe and Logan have already started down the alley. You don't want to be left behind.

To shut the back door, turn to page 84.
To follow Chloe and Logan, turn to page 88.

Even though the man inside the station wanted to throw you to the wolves, you can't leave the door open. You ease your way back around the zombies and step up to the door. You grab the handle and swing the door shut as quietly as you can, but the click of the bolt locking in place is almost deafening in the silence.

The zombies look up at the same time. Without hesitation, you dash forward, hoping to get past the zombies before they can get to their feet. It almost works, but the zombie closest to you grabs your right hand. Before you pull free, the zombie sinks its teeth into the fleshy part of your palm. You rip your hand free, backpedaling while clutching your bitten hand.

You catch up to Chloe and Logan. Their eyes immediately fall to your bleeding hand.

"Oh no! Tell me you snagged it on the fence ..." says Chloe.

You try to respond, but your words catch in your throat. The three of you just stand there, looking at your hand.

"C'mon," you say finally. "The zombies are going to catch up to us any minute. Let's see if we can reach the evacuation zone."

Chloe and Logan look at each other. You know what the gaze means—they know you won't be evacuated because you've been bitten. Not knowing what else to do, the three of you head south.

You walk through the empty streets without saying a word. Chloe's gasp breaks the silence as a group of zombies wanders into the intersection in front of you.

"Look!" says Logan, pointing past the zombies to a line of military vehicles. "That must be the evacuation zone!"

"Then let's make a run for it," you say.

Turn the page.

You could easily sprint past the zombies, but a voice booms over a PA system. "Stop where you are!"

You stop in your tracks and throw your arms in the air. Chloe and Logan do the same. But the zombies are only 30 feet away and moving in.

"We should rush forward with our arms up," says Chloe.

"If we run ahead, we'll be shot," says Logan. "We have to stay put."

To move toward the evacuation zone, turn to page 92.

To stay where you are, turn to page 93.

You follow Logan and Chloe and put some distance between you and the police station.

"We should try to reach the evacuation zone," says Chloe. "Let's head northwest."

It's hard to imagine that the streets were filled with screams and panic not more than an hour ago. The zombies have followed the crowd somewhere else, and the streets are empty. You jog down the sidewalk, keeping an eye out for anything strange. After a half-hour, you reach a barricade of orange mesh fencing and heavily armored military vehicles.

"FREEZE!"

A soldier 50 feet away aims the barrel of an assault rifle at you. Your knees buckle as your hands shoot in the air. "We're not zombies!" you yell.

The soldier keeps his distance but waves the barrel of the gun, indicating that you should follow him. You go into a tent where a man in a lab coat checks you for bites. He nods to the soldier, and you're pushed through an open gate where you meet up with Chloe and Logan. The soldier takes you to an open field with several helicopters.

"We have to get out of here NOW!" yells one of the soldiers. "This whole town is going to be leveled in 20 minutes!"

"What? I'm not leaving until I know my parents are OK!" you shout.

Without a word, he hoists you onto one of the helicopters. Moments later, the helicopter takes flight. Twenty minutes later, a bright light blinds you, and the helicopter shakes. You see a mushroom cloud hovering over the city. You can only hope your parents made it out alive.

THE END

To follow another path, turn to page 9.
To learn more about zombies, turn to page 101.

You head down the hallway and into the main room. Three of the people are already on the ground, surrounded by zombies.

Two of the windows have shattered, and zombies have pulled the bearded man halfway out one of the windows. A woman has one of the man's feet under each arm and is trying to pull him back in. You rush over and pull on one of the man's legs. You and the woman synchronize your pulls, and on the fourth one, the man tumbles back inside. However, he has bites and scratches all over his arms and face.

You and the woman turn to run, but it's too late. The hallway is cut off, and zombies are starting to come in through the window. Your eyes meet the woman's, and you huddle together as the zombies close in.

THE END

To follow another path, turn to page 9.
To learn more about zombies, turn to page 101.

The zombies are already breathing down your neck. You have to move fast. You keep your arms raised as you walk briskly ahead, around the zombies.

Chloe lets out a scream at the sound of a gunshot. You spin your head around, dreading what you'll see. A zombie that had caught Chloe falls to the ground.

You turn around and keep moving ahead slowly as more gunshots ring out. Within a minute, several armed soldiers rush toward you, guns raised.

"Have any of you been scratched or bitten by a zombie?" asks one of the soldiers.

Chloe and Logan stay silent. You know that if you tell them the truth, you'll get left behind. But you don't want to endanger any of the other survivors, especially your friends.

To show the soldier your bite, turn to page 94.
To lie to the soldier, turn to page 97.

"Let's sit tight," you say. "I'm sure they'll send out help soon."

You huddle together with Chloe and Logan as the zombies get closer. In less than a minute, four armed soldiers run out to meet you. Three of the soldiers fire on the closest zombies, and the fourth walks up to meet you.

"Follow me and we'll get you to a helicopter for evacuation."

The soldier turns and takes two steps before stopping short. The other soldiers' gunfire has drawn a horde of zombies from all directions. The soldiers back in around you, their guns swinging to aim at a new zombie each time one falls. You hear the click of an empty chamber, followed by another, then another. You follow the soldiers as they try to charge back to the base, but you're soon overwhelmed by waves of zombies.

THE END

To follow another path, turn to page 9.
To learn more about zombies, turn to page 101.

"Yes, sir," you reply, holding out your arm. "I was bitten on the hand."

He steps toward you and looks at the bite mark on your palm. "How long ago?" he asks.

"About an hour ago."

"That may give us enough time," he says. Before you ask what he means, two soldiers grab you by the arms.

The soldiers lead you into a tent and hoist you onto a table. They tie your hands and feet down as a man in a biohazard suit walks up to the table. Your eyes drop to the syringe in his hand. The needle is longer than any you've seen before.

"My name is Dr. Bachmann," the man says. "Congratulations—you will be one of the first people to try the experimental antidote."

It's a good thing you walked instead of drove. You would still be stuck in traffic right now. At least now you have a chance of recovery.

Turn the page.

Dr. Bachmann plunges the needle into your arm. The pain is even worse than you imagined. After he removes the needle, a soldier covers your arm with a bandage. He walks over to another person in a biohazard suit. "Now we wait," he says. "We should know if the antidote works within 48 hours."

Several soldiers come in and hook you up to machines that monitor your vital signs. Over the next two days, Dr. Bachmann comes in to check on you often. Soldiers give you food and water, but your arms and legs remain tied to the table.

On the third day, Dr. Bachmann comes in wearing a lab coat—the biohazard suit is gone. "Good news," he says. "The antidote is a success—we caught it in time. You will be free to leave soon."

A sigh of relief rushes out of you. You can't wait to see your friends and family again.

THE END

To follow another path, turn to page 9.
To learn more about zombies, turn to page 101.

"No, none of us have been bitten," you tell the soldier.

"All right," he says. "Then follow me."

He leads you to a large tent where hundreds of other survivors are waiting in a line. "They need to get your names and some other information before you're allowed to leave," he says. Then he abruptly walks out of the tent.

Logan eyes you warily. "I can't believe you lied to him," he says through gritted teeth. "I'm sorry you were bitten, but you're endangering everyone."

You don't know what to say. He's right, but you were scared. You hang your head and step ahead as the line moves.

"I feel okay, though. Maybe I won't turn," you reply, hopefully.

Turn the page.

After more than two hours of waiting, you're starting to near the front. Chloe puts her arm around your shoulder and gives you a hug. "Everything will be OK, you'll see," she says with a forced smile.

Suddenly, a woman next to you backs away and screams. She points at your bitten hand, and armed soldiers come running.

Before you can react, your arms are pinned behind you and secured with rope. One of the men covers your eyes with a blindfold and drags you out of the tent. After a short ride in the back seat of a car, you're carried into a building and tossed into a room. The door slams shut, and everything goes dark.

You scream for help, but your cries only echo back at you. The room must be solid concrete. You spend the next several hours trying to loosen the rope, but it's no use.

You shudder as a strange warmth rushes through your body. Your forehead is on fire, and nausea hits you like a battering ram. You start to cough in violent fits, which causes you to tip onto your side. Drool slides out of your mouth and pools on the floor as your vision starts to blur. That's when the hunger starts in. Before long, you'll be one of the undead.

THE END

To follow another path, turn to page 9.
To learn more about zombies, turn to page 101.

ZOMBIES: PAST AND PRESENT

From George A. Romero's long list of zombie movies to Max Brooks' detailed analysis of the undead, these brain-loving monsters are a hit in pop culture today. But the idea of zombies started in Haitian culture. Legend has it that voodoo witch doctors—also called *bokors*—could turn people into zombies in a process called zombification. A person going through this process would die and be brought back to life. Then they would be under the control of the *bokor*.

The Haitian voodoo zombies gained popularity in the 1930s and 1940s. People were gripped—and terrified—by movies such as *The White Zombie* and *I Walked with a Zombie*. The films featured voodoo practices and people using mind control to command the zombies. Over time, the concept of mind control dropped out of many zombie stories. Today, a zombie's actions are driven by only one thing—the need to feed.

Skeptics aren't convinced that zombies exist or that they could one day roam the streets looking to feed. Yet there are examples of "zombies" in nature. The fungus Ophiocordyceps unilaterius can turn insects into creatures that behave like zombies from the Haitian voodoo culture. The spores of the fungus are parasites that affect its host's brain. The mind-controlled insect climbs to higher ground and clings to the underside of a leaf before it dies. A stalk full of fungus spores erupts from the ant's head like an antenna. The spores spread in the wind, waiting to turn other insects into mindless slaves.

One species of bird mimics another type of zombie—the brain-hungry type! The bird Parus Major will hunt down a bat, crack open its skull, and eat its brain. But they aren't the only animals feasting on brains. Certain species of tree kangaroos, tapeworms, and even chipmunks have been known to dine on the brains of other creatures. The scariest part is that they eat only the brain and discard the body when they're done.

These creatures definitely have zombie-like qualities, but the question remains: Can people really become zombies? One of the most common traits of a zombie—to bite anything within its reach—has been compared to an animal with rabies. But scientists say the rabies virus has a long way to go before it can start a zombie-like outbreak. The virus would have to multiply faster and affect more cells in the human body. It would also have to spread from person to person more quickly. Instead of taking one to three months to affect the host, it would need to happen in a matter of days.

Even if the rabies virus could do all of that, it would still have to mutate. The new virus would attack the brain but still allow the person (or zombie) to move and function. Right now, the rabies virus causes brain damage that eventually leads to death.

Still, past epidemics have shown the potential for viruses to spread quickly, which is a concern if a virus could trigger something like a zombie outbreak. And although it's not likely that zombies would rise from a natural virus, some undead experts claim a synthetic virus made in a laboratory could do the trick. However, scientists would have to solve the issues facing the natural viruses before they could make it work. Although there are many theories about how zombies could become a reality, scientists remain unconvinced that a zombie uprising could actually happen.

In the highly unlikely case of a zombie apocalypse, the Centers for Disease Control and Prevention actually does have a plan. As with any disease, scientists there would try to find out where it started, how it is transmitted, and how to treat victims. They would also assist in setting up quarantine zones to keep the outbreak from spreading. So whether you think zombies are made up or if you are just waiting for the undead to roam the world, it's better to be prepared!

ZOMBIE APOCALYPSE
SURVIVAL GUIDE

The Pentagon and Centers for Disease Control and Prevention have used the popularity of zombies to spread awareness of disaster preparedness. People can take some of the same steps to prepare for a zombie apocalypse as they would natural disasters.

Make an evacuation plan and pick a place to meet up with your family. You'll also need a zombie survival kit, including:

*WATER

*NON-PERISHABLE FOOD AND A CAN OPENER

*A FIRST-AID KIT AND ANY MEDICATION YOU MAY NEED

*TOOLS OR SUPPLIES THAT HAVE MANY USES, SUCH AS A SWISS ARMY KNIFE AND DUCT TAPE

*FLASHLIGHTS

*A BATTERY-POWERED RADIO (GET THE LATEST INFO ABOUT THE ZOMBIE OUTBREAK!)

*BATTERIES

*A VARIETY OF CLOTHES (FOR ALL TYPES OF WEATHER)

*BLANKETS

This list is just a start. Talk to your family about other items you could include. Just remember to pack only what you need. You don't want to be weighed down if you need to make a quick getaway!

TEN TIPS
TO SURVIVE A ZOMBIE APOCALYPSE

- There's no use playing dead when a zombie's near. The scent of flesh will lead it right to you.

- Be aware of your surroundings. Always have several exits in mind in case zombies cut off your main escape route.

- Avoid heavily populated areas. Zombies are attracted to noise and people, so you'll have the most luck in an isolated area.

- There IS some safety in numbers, but smaller groups have a better chance of remaining unseen.

- Zombies are deadly but slow. Instead of taking on a zombie in close quarters, try to outrun them.

- If you have to fight, remember that a zombie can get by without an arm or a leg. To kill a zombie, aim for the head.

- Travel during the day. It's easier to avoid zombies when you can see them coming. Besides, zombies gain the upper hand in the dark with their sense of smell.

- Stay on your guard. You'll need to rest up, but make sure one person is always on the lookout.

- You never know when your barricade might break down! Keep your survival kit packed and ready to go at a moment's notice.

- If you're able to hunker down somewhere, make a sign that can be seen from the sky. You don't want to miss out on your chance of being rescued.

GLOSSARY

ANTIDOTE (AN-ti-dote)—something that stops a poison from working

APOCALYPSE (uh-PAH-kuh-lips)—an event involving serious destruction and possibly the end of the world in its current state

BARRICADE (BARE-uh-cayd)—something set up to block passage into an area

EVACUATE (i-VA-kyuh-wayt)—to leave an area during a time of danger

GNASH (NASH)—to grind together, usually with teeth

HORDE (HORD)—a large group

HOST (HOHST)—a living thing from which another living thing gets nutrition

ISOLATED (EYE-suh-lay-tuhd)—the condition of being alone

MUTATE (MYOO-tayt)—to change in some way

PARASITE (PAIR-uh-site)—an animal or plant that lives on or inside another animal or plant and causes harm

QUARANTINE (KWOR-uhn-teen)—to keep a person, animal, or plant away from others to stop a disease from spreading

RABIES (RAY-beez)—a deadly disease that people and animals can get from the bite of an infected animal

SEDATE (si-DATE)—to make someone calm or sleepy, especially by giving the person medicine

SKEPTIC (SKEP-tik)—a person who questions things that other people believe in

SOLEMN (SOL-uhm)—very serious

SYNTHETIC (sin-THET-ik)—something that is artificial or manufactured rather than found in nature

SYRINGE (suh-RINJ)—a tube with a plunger and a hollow needle; licensed medical workers use syringes to inject medicine into patients

VOODOO (VOO-doo)—a religion that began in Africa that combines Catholicism with various mystical and magical beliefs and practices

ZOMBIFICATION (zom-buh-fuh-KAY-shuhn)—the process of becoming a zombie

READ MORE

Dakota, Heather. *Zombie Apocalypse Survival Guide.*
New York: Tangerine Press, an imprint of Scholastic Inc., 2013.

Jones, Jen. *The Girls' Guide to Zombies: Everything Vital
about These Undead Monsters.* North Mankato, Minn.:
Capstone Publishers, 2011.

INTERNET SITES

Use FactHound to find Internet sites related to this book.
All of the sites on FactHound have been researched by our staff.

Here's all you do:
Visit *www.facthound.com*
Type in this code: 9781491458525

AUTHOR

Anthony Wacholtz is a writer and editor with a love of things that
go bump in the night. He lives with his wife, Katrina, and dog, Max,
in Rochester, Minnesota, where he is ready and waiting for the
zombie apocalypse.

ILLUSTRATOR

James Nathan attended Worcester College of Art and Design in
England and received a degree in Illustration at Cardiff School of
Art and Design. His artwork is mostly fantasy and science fiction
based, inspired by Pixar illustrations as well as the artist Dan LuVisi.
James lives in Bristol, England, with his girlfriend and cat. In his
spare time he enjoys making music, as well as music videos.